Kat,

I hope t̶ ~~G000135268~~ ng amazing.

I wanted to share this book with you because I never would have been in a place to write it, if it weren't for you and your Instagram Makeover course.

Thanks for changing my life.

Lots of love,

Raina ☺

A Little Book to Change the World:

A Practical Guide to the Opinions of Others

By Raina Kropp

Little Golden Butterfly LLC.
San Diego, CA

Little Golden Butterfly LLC.
www.LittleGoldenButterfly.com

Special discounts are available on quantity purchases by corporations, associations, and others. For details, contact the publisher.

Library of Congress Control Number: 2023904279

A Little Book to Change the World:
A Practical Guide to the Opinions of Others – 1st ed.

ISBN 979-8-9879242-1-1 (paperback)
ISBN 979-8-9879242-0-4 (hardback)
ISBN 979-8-9879242-2-8 (kindle ebook)

To my amazing sister, Kelsi.

I couldn't have done it without you.
I love you.

Contents

CHAPTER 1

How It Started

It started with a comment on one of my Instagram posts. Someone accused me of being a fake and buying my followers.

Now, to some of you this may not seem like that big of a deal or even an insult of sorts.

For me though, I had spent the past year pouring everything I had into my business.

I worked so hard to start and grow my business, which was run through my Instagram account.

The post the person commented on was one of the few times I posted about how proud I was of what I accomplished so far.

When the person made a comment saying that I had bought followers, it felt like they were telling me that they were skeptical that I had really accomplished all that much and that I was really trying to scam or trick people.

I couldn't stop crying because my feelings were so hurt, and I couldn't understand why someone would attack me like that.

Unfortunately, this was not the first time someone had posted negative comments on my page. I had started a new business, and in that first year or two, I received a number of comments that hurt my feelings.

Things like, "Do you not realize how dumb you look doing this?" or "Cringe."

There were a lot of hateful comments I just deleted and people I just blocked. I think it's the nature of being on social media and people feeling fearless behind a keyboard. People are willing to say a lot of mean and hateful things.

Even when I would try to brush it off, I would still think about those comments for days on end. For my own well-being, I had to find a way to deal with it.

What I didn't realize is that in learning to deal with this, I was applying the prior 15+ years of conflict management tools I had learned in the corporate world as a Human Resources Business Partner, a role that involved lots of conflict management between employees, managers, and leadership.

From that experience, I was able to come up with a method that helped me make peace with the hateful comments being made by strangers online.

And from there, I realized it helped not just with strangers but also with loved ones who sometimes have unfair judgments of us or that we may have conflict with.

And so, The RAINA Method was born.

I believe this method is needed now more than ever.

So many harsh words have been exchanged lately...

On the Internet,
In person,
In the media.

And at first,
They upset me,
Made me mad,
Saddened me,

And lately inspired me.

Because I think it could be better.

I believe we could be kinder.
I believe there could be less hurt feelings out there.

And less hurting in general.

I believe many of us have never been given the skills, or the tools, to do that.

That's why I wrote this book.

A Little Book to Change the World,

Because I love you.

And I love the World.

CHAPTER 2

How It Works

When that random person accused me of being fake and buying followers, I couldn't believe it.

My first reaction was to try and make sense of it.

Internally, I screamed, "Why would someone say that about me? I can't believe it. It doesn't make any sense!"

And the more I couldn't make sense of it, the more I got upset.

I felt attacked. I felt like the victim of a cruel, unfair judgment.

And when we feel attacked, many of us instinctively go back into our caveman fight or flight mode, which in a society without sabertooth tigers, may not be the most evolved way to respond.

When we go into fight or flight mode, oxygen, nutrients, and blood flow are redirected from our brain to our muscles in preparation for stress. This state was ideal in a time when you had to run away or fight prehistoric predators, but may not be ideal for today's world or an ideal state to think rationally.

What do these states look like today?

Instead of fleeing or fighting prehistoric predators, we are having non-verbal and verbal interactions with people in person and online. We either flee the source of the verbal attack, or we fight back.

1. We flee, feel hurt, and go lick our wounds in private or in the company of those we think will support us and our point of view.

2. We fight back by vilifying and invalidating the source/ the person who said it [usually by putting that person down in some way].

These instinctual responses are outdated and highly ineffectual in today's online world.

The Fight response can quickly escalate into hurt feelings, hateful words, and in the worst case, physical violence against another human being, which we should avoid at all costs.

Along with the Fight response, the most common desire is to not only fight but to defend ourselves by convincing the other party they are wrong.

[For example - Me trying to comment back to that user that I did, in fact, not buy my followers.]

In other words, when we disagree with someone, it's a natural response or desire, to be "right", and to prove the other person "wrong".

This innately causes a Winner/Loser situation.

And no one wants to be a loser in a fighting situation.

The magic is when we realize that it's not about winning/losing or being right/wrong.

There is a 🔽
3RD OPTION.

The RAINA Method.

Let's review using the example from before.

Incident:
Someone accused me of buying followers.

Me:
Instead of crying, lamenting about why they would accuse me of that, or getting into a verbal spat with them, let's see the RAINA Method applied.

Internal Dialogue after reading the comment accusing me of buying followers:

"That totally makes sense. Of course, someone might think that.

Fewer people liked some of my posts than they might imagine for someone with my size following.

Conclusion: this person must be buying followers.

They must believe they need to point this out to others so that they know I am a scam. It is their duty."

That's basically the dialogue in my head. I put myself in their shoes and explain to myself why their actions 1000% make perfect sense.

My first response is to essentially accept that their actions are completely reasonable.

Then, because they are completely reasonable, I am in a better mindset to realize I don't have to:

- lash out;
- get defensive;
- jump to conclusions; or
- be mean.

I know I haven't bought followers and that's all that matters.

Now there's a little more finesse around this technique than that quick summary.

But basically, I dig deep to understand and come up with a reasonable reason why they would do/say this.

I DO NOT have to agree with it,

BUT I DO have to challenge myself to truly understand their human experience.

And once I can do that, I can respond in a way that

ALLOWS THE BEST POSSIBLE OUTCOME FOR ALL PARTIES.

What I discovered is that making peace and dealing with social media hate online uses much of the same principles as making peace and dealing with conflict involving loved ones in person. Some common goals are:

1. To make peace with what happened internally for myself; and
2. To be as productive as possible in that given situation.

Sometimes, it's going to be sharing a thoughtful opinion, actively listening and talking in person, and validating each other's opinions. And sometimes, it's going to be about walking away and choosing not to engage in the situation.

There doesn't have to be a perfect resolution, because that's not always possible. The goal of this method is to help you feel more peaceful and calm about the situation so that you can take action in an intentional and thoughtful way you can be proud of.

Pausing to take a step back to get a view of the bigger picture is going to yield much better long-term results over the temporary personal satisfaction of just saying whatever you want and potentially hurting others and yourself in the process.

Is the RAINA Method always easy to apply? Absolutely not.

For most, it is against our gut instinct and first impulse.

BUT, is it worth it to master this technique through practice and repetition?

Yes! 100%!

We need this method now more than ever to protect our mental health and not let ourselves be defined or valued based on the opinions of others.

And, those who truly embrace this method of conflict resolution will see their lives begin to change in miraculous ways.

CHAPTER 3

The RAINA Method

The RAINA Method

R - Assume they're **Reasonable** and valid
A - **Amplify** their position
I - **Inspect** and investigate your biases
N - Uncover your **Naked Truth** - What do I really want? What is a mutually beneficial goal?
A - Take **Aligned Action**

First, let's break down each step.

R - *Assume they're* ***Reasonable*** *and valid*

When you find yourself feeling attacked or in conflict, the first step is to assume the other person's opinion is reasonable and valid in their paradigm.

In contrast, when you label someone as unreasonable or rude, you inadvertently think of them as the bad guy or the attacker, and thus you conveniently justify defending yourself and attacking them back.

So, labeling them as reasonable, is the first step to humanizing them again.

Reasonable in this method means that, based on their morals, beliefs, and life experiences, this is what they know to be true and right.

Instead of thinking, "What is wrong with them? How can they possibly think that?"

Try saying to yourself, "Of course that makes sense. It's totally reasonable that from their point of view they would think that."

Something about categorizing an unwanted opinion as a reasonable reaction, sets us up to react in a reasonable way.

Of course, maybe you don't want to react reasonably, but that's a different story.

This is not about agreeing with them. You can understand someone, empathize even, without agreeing with them.

This is more about keeping your own peace of mind in a world full of noise.

If you're constantly triggered into anger simply by someone else's opinion, then you are not in control of your own life.

True peace and freedom is knowing yourself and knowing that no one can control your emotions and actions. They say emotions are contagious, and that negativity has a way of spreading. When someone doesn't feel good, they often say or do mean things, because they want you to feel what they are feeling.

Don't fall for transference. Protect yourself from absorbing that energy.

This technique will help you do just that.

Please note: the goal of this method is not to minimize harmful statements others make or to minimize or invalidate your feelings. The goal of this step specifically is to put yourself in the best possible head space to figure out how to proceed in a situation after comments have been made.

A - *Amplify* their position

Now that you have assumed that the other person's thoughts can be valid and reasonable, it is time to explore their world.

Ask yourself, "In their world, how would this be a simple truth?"

Sometimes, I say, "In their world, obviously that makes sense. If I grew up with friends and family who taught me that, and the only life experience I've had has not shown me otherwise, then why would I believe differently?"

Get curious. Ponder things about their childhood. About their daily life. Their daily struggles.

Ask yourself, "Why might that be?" "What would it have to look like for that person to say and act that way?"

Think about their age, their race, their health conditions, their residence, and how that might affect their interactions with others.

For example, I found myself getting upset by someone's posts I follow on Instagram.

They were saying how all corporations are evil and how they are always trying to take advantage of employees.

I spent 15 years in Corporate Human Resources, so initially, I was feeling super defensive.

Because from my point of view, I spent much of my career looking out for employees and doing my best by them.

But then I took a step back, and asked myself, "Why would this be their truth? What would their personal history and experience have to be for them to hate corporations so much?"

The answer wasn't too hard to find.

This person had been a former trial lawyer for wronged employees.

So for the 15 years, I was on the Corporate HR side looking out for employees, all they saw were the companies that had maliciously wronged their employees.

I paused and reflected on that.

If my experience had been theirs and all I had dealt with for a decade was defending employees against companies that had actually done their employees wrong, then I might vilify all companies as well.

Now that I understood that, I realized I didn't have to feel defensive.

Of course, their opinions on corporations may not come from their work as an attorney, but by trying to put myself in their position, it allows me to see a different perspective and come to terms with the possible reasons for our different opinions.

I ultimately decided to unfollow them. And it wasn't a big deal.

I didn't have to stew over or ruminate over their opinion.

And though I did unfollow them, I didn't feel the need to comment on their post and tell them any of that. Because I understood why they might feel that way.

Each of us has a unique life experience to lend depth and breadth to how we view an issue.

Sometimes, amplifying their position will be really hard. You may really struggle with putting yourself in their shoes and understanding what in their lives could make them do or say something. Especially when you try this for the first time, it might feel awkward and unnatural.

Start with something small.

Always assume there is an answer that makes complete sense in their world.

It's just a matter of figuring out what that is. And the more you practice this, the less sarcastic the effort might become.

If you find yourself getting stumped, check out the Key Takeaways section at the end of this book for some additional exercises and questions.

I know at first, it may be almost begrudgingly.

However, the more you genuinely try to understand and put yourself in the other person's shoes, the easier it will become.

And the less upset and stressed you will be when faced with opposing viewpoints.

Remember, you're not doing this to ultimately agree with the other person, only to empathize and understand them so that you can process and respond to the situation in a way that will allow for the best outcome possible.

Sometimes, I will even imagine hugging the thought bubble that holds their opinion and gently placing it down to simply observe it.

The thought then just becomes a little puzzle, a tiny game for me to figure out and understand.

Sometimes, I find it easier to tackle if I make a game out of it.

Like, how do I come up with the most reasonable and plausible circumstances that make those beliefs true?

This gamification helps me think more creatively and keeps frustration at bay.

Please note: Everything you come up with in this step to illustrate the other person's world are:

- THEORIES;
- GUESSES; or
- HYPOTHESES.

Even if you are using this method with someone you know in real life.

Now, when it comes to strangers, or someone you'll never have contact with again, it's okay to leave it as a theory.

However, when it comes to the real relationships that are important to you, it is important to come from a place of **NOTHING** is fact, unless it is validated by the other person.

So even if you believe that you have correctly amplified their position in your mind, if it is about a person you have a real relationship with, be sure to follow up with a thoughtful conversation to share and validate your assumptions.

For example, if you're processing something that happened between you and your partner. That should be very different than if you were just processing something that happened between you and a random person online.

Let's say:

My partner is quiet throughout dinner and doesn't say much before going to bed. And this is out of character.

I might have thought that my partner had a long day at work and is just tired, BUT I should bring it up with my partner later to validate that assumption.

Because I value the relationship with my partner.

It's dangerous to always make up reasons for someone else's actions because then you risk being in an echo chamber of your own making. Instead of responding to truth, you are responding to assumptions.

Never assume. Always stay curious.
You might be surprised by what you find.

I - *Inspect* and investigate your biases

Now that you have amplified their position and pondered why they might think the way they do, let's look at our own biases.

Often, these can be lenses through which we see the world without even being aware of them.

What is obvious to you is not obvious to someone else who grew up with different parents, in a different neighborhood, in a different country, with different friends, a different culture, and a different set of norms.

Often we have biases that we aren't even aware of because we are not exposed to or surrounded by people with life experiences vastly different from our own.

We tend to hang out and surround ourselves with people who look and think like us. Part of the reason why is that we are so quick to assign likability attributes based on whether someone's opinion is aligned with ours.

It can feel like the easiest course of action to be pulled to people who think just like us, however, it's important to know that there is a depth and breadth of infinite knowledge and experience to be explored in this world.

Learning from others, especially those who have different opinions and experiences than our own can be beneficial.

If you only surround yourself with people who are like you, it can unknowingly limit possible outcomes, resolutions, or new experiences.

What if we could be around others vastly different from ourselves, enjoy each other's company and get along without being triggered because someone has a different opinion?

Part of achieving that will be identifying your own biases in different situations and around different opinions.

Ask yourself these questions to uncover some of the common biases that arise when we disagree with an opinion:

- Am I trying to prove I'm right?
- If I'm not trying to defend myself, is there some truth to the statement?
- Do I feel like I need to defend my behavior?
- Am I looking for validation?
- Am I carrying any shame around this? Around being this or around doing this?
- If I'm not ashamed of my behavior, can I just own this truth?
- If I wasn't feeling attacked, how would I respond?
- If what they're saying didn't comment on my life choices, then how would I feel?
- If what they're saying is true, does it imply I'm a bad person?
- Am I responding in a passive-aggressive or sarcastic manner?
- What is most important to me when making a decision?
- What kinds of information or opinions do I value? What kinds do I dismiss? And why?

- What are my main sources of information? What news sources, podcasts, and people do I listen to? Do those sources of information have people or entities that they criticize or dismiss? Have I watched/read those other sources of information directly with an open mind?
- What kind of mood am I in right now? What state of mind? Am I unhappy right now? Is my mood clouding my response?
- Am I making a blanket statement or generalization about a group of people?
- Am I blaming or defending a group of people?

If the answer is yes to any of these questions, then you might want to pause before responding.

The pause is to allow you to understand any biases you may have clouding your response.

When we have biases, we might say things we don't even really mean because we're caught up in the heat of the moment.

If we are too focused on defending ourselves against attack, we can actually lose sight of the real issue.

In getting caught up in defending our actions, we actually lose our best chance of securing an optimal outcome.

Sometimes, it's us, not them, who have a problem or blind spot. It can be hard to see ourselves objectively.

Without even realizing it, most of the content and people we are exposed to are innately biased, because we tend to seek out people and information that aligns with our opinions and values.

The Instagram Algorithm, for instance, will fill your feed with people who think like you do, like the same things and have overlapping interests.

Not to say it's good or bad, just know that you sometimes won't even realize you're in an echo chamber.

An echo chamber happens when you hang out with a group of people you easily get along with and with whom you have a lot of the same interests and opinions. Most of the opinions you have are then "echoed" back to you over and over, which reinforces your belief system that everyone probably has these opinions, because you have less and less exposure to other outside opinions.

So much of what we consume nowadays is through recommendations from friends, family, and influencers. These tend to be recommendations to people who think similarly to us.

To truly understand your own biases and fairly identify where you might be in an echo chamber, you will need to challenge yourself to seek out other opinions and information that are different or even in conflict with what you "know" to be true.

Otherwise, you are really just consuming information you already know and gaining no new knowledge or perspective.

When you disagree with another person, it may be because your current opinions might be based on a small sample of information that does not include the whole picture. To truly understand the other person, you may need to investigate or seek to find what the full spectrum is out there, in order to have a clear view of the picture.

And you shouldn't just accept information or recommendations of others and adopt them as your own without testing them out yourself.

For instance, if you get your news from primarily one cable news network or website, perhaps there are people or news sources that they do not speak highly of or discredit. It may be beneficial to sometimes seek out those people or news sources and listen to them yourself with an open mind.

Or, instead of one specific media news source, maybe you found yourself often relying on a particular person in your life that you love and trust to give you the news.

I'm guilty of this. I personally stopped reading and listening to the news years ago because it would upset me and put me in a negative mood.

So many times, I would rely on my husband to convey to me news and politics that were most relevant or pressing. I love and respect him, and in most cases our opinions align, but I also recognize he may be unknowingly filtering information for me.

When really important issues come up, it's on me to do my own research and seek out multiple and varying sources of information, if I want to truly understand the whole picture.

It would be a shame to miss out on those unfiltered pieces of information because I had unrealized biases at work.

Here are some questions to ask yourself to aid in objectivity and hopefully neutralize some of those biases:

- Have I attacked or blamed a person or group of people for something?
- Am I willing to concede to being wrong?
- Do I have to be right?
- Am I afraid of being wrong?
- Am I too attached to a specific outcome to be objective?
- Have I considered the state/country infrastructure, laws or systems in place that might be playing a large role in the other person's world? Or play a large role in mine?
- Is there a power or privilege differential between me and the other person? Do I have shame around that difference? If I have power and privilege, can I own/ use it to both our advantage?

You can tell biases are at work when you start talking to your friends and in your word choice, you start to talk about people, with different opinions, as "them" or an outside group to which you do not belong. Try to catch yourself if you find yourself labeling others, using stereotypes, or making widespread generalizations.

This is a sign of your biases at work.

Any phrasing that indicates a group other than one you belong to has the chance of dehumanizing the other person/ group and allows you to take less than kind action.

When we make the other person an "other", we have the potential to cause hurt and shame, then we become part of the hateful cycle. We add to the hate instead of diffusing it.

Once you are aware of these biases or tendencies, you can act intentionally and make a choice.
And in choice, you hold power.

Don't be discouraged if this is hard. It's a process. The more you do it, the easier it will get and the better you will become.

N - Uncover Your **Naked Truth** - What do I really want? What is a mutually beneficial goal?

At this point, you have assumed their thoughts are valid, amplified their position, and thought through your own biases.

Use what you've learned so far to strip away your own biases from the situation. This will help you uncover your Naked Truth, which is a raw, plain, and unbiased truth.

This unbiased truth is something you can admit to yourself when you're not trying to be cool or righteous. An unbiased truth is something you can see and hold when you're not trying to prove or defend yourself or your lifestyle.

Your Naked Truth will be a guiding light. Revealing it will help you decide what you really want out of the situation and what you want for others. It's a truth unclouded by biases.

It's a good thing if you feel vulnerable at this stage. It means you did a thorough job amplifying their position and stripping away your own biases.

Now you can see the true picture and make an intentional decision. What do you really want to get from this interaction?

Let me illustrate a good example by sharing a quick story.

I went to the Doctor's for a routine procedure once. As I was waiting in the room for the doctor to arrive, a male nurse came in and laid out the equipment on a tray.

He then left, and a little while later, another nurse, this one female, came in, looking at the tray.

She shook her head and sighed heavily, then turned to me and said, "I'm sorry. He's new."

She then put away half of the tools on the tray and replaced them with other equipment, all while mumbling to herself about his incompetence.

I want to pause here for a second and reflect.

I remember having an epiphany at that moment.

I had never really understood what my boss meant until that very moment when he used to say "My reputation is your reputation, and your reputation is my reputation."

Because I used to do the same thing to my coworkers sometimes when they dropped the ball on stuff. Looking back,

I thought I was empathizing with the internal customer, but in letting that person know it was a coworker's fault something wasn't getting done, I wasn't really shifting the blame. I was cementing the blame for my entire department and casting doubt on our competency as a whole.

Going back to this interaction at the doctor's office, it made me realize that the nurse's reputation was her colleague's reputation, the doctor's reputation, and the hospital's reputation.

Because after that nurse switched the equipment, I was feeling very insecure as the patient and felt nervous about the upcoming procedure because of it.

Here's how it could have gone differently:

If that female nurse had applied the RAINA Method, she might have paused when seeing the tray.

I imagine the inner dialogue could have looked like this:

"Of course that makes sense. It's totally reasonable that from Bobby's point of view, he would think that those were the tools needed for today's procedure.

Perhaps in his training, I wasn't as thorough or detailed in explaining why, in this case, slightly different tools should be used.

Maybe there's an opportunity here to improve our training. Maybe I can add this to the training manual or create some type of cheat sheet or reference card, so it's more obvious in the future.

I might be a little biased since I've been doing this for years, and I take for granted that I easily know what to do and how to prepare.

How should I handle this in front of the patient?

I need to talk to Bobby, so that moving forward he knows the correct tools to lay out and why. I can pull him aside later and tell him.

For now, I need to consider the patient.

I want them to feel confident going into the procedure, and how I react right now will directly impact how they are feeling.

Given that, I'll just confidently walk up to the tray and replace those tools like it's no big deal.

Then I'll smile, tell them it looks like we're just about ready, and that the doctor will be in here shortly."

So you see here, a naked truth for the female nurse might be that she's partially responsible for why Bobby laid out the wrong tools.

As mentioned previously, identifying your naked truth can make you feel vulnerable. One thing that I have discovered that makes it a little easier is to have empathy for yourself.

Empathy has been shown to be the most effective method of putting ourselves in a receptive and open mindset.

If you can speak kindly to yourself and give grace to yourself, you'll be in a better mindset to speak kindly and give grace to others.

By giving herself grace, the female nurse would also be able to see the whole picture and consider that a mutually beneficial goal not only means beneficial to her and Bobby **but also for the patient.**

Ask yourself these questions to see how close you are to the naked truth and finding a mutually beneficial solution for all involved:

- Will other people be affected by how I react?
- How could I see the situation differently?
- Am I open to a solution I cannot yet see?
- Am I solving the issue to the benefit of both parties? How about for the benefit of all parties affected?
- Are both parties better off than they were before our interaction?
- Am I considering the larger/whole picture?
- Am I considering the infrastructure of our society and culture?

Okay, so what do we do now?

A - Take **Aligned Action**

Now that we:

- Understand the other person better;
- Understand ourselves better;
- Understand our naked truth; and
- Have come up with a mutually beneficial solution;

We can take action.

In the last example we discussed, that action was to confidently walk up to the tray and replace the tools like it was no big deal.

It was also an intentional choice to pull Bobby aside and let him know in confidence what he did wrong instead of correcting him in public or in front of an audience.

There may also be times when you choose not to talk to Bobby. There have been times in my past when I was not able to work it out with a coworker. That's okay, especially in cases where the other person is not open to dialogue.

This method will not always result in a perfect outcome, however, it should help you process the situation in an intentional and thoughtful way so that you can have peace around the decision you make.

Sometimes that decision may be to not talk to the other person. In that instance, you won't be able to validate your assumptions around their position, but you can still make peace on your side with your thoughts and actions based on the information you have.

I also know we can sometimes daydream of the perfect putdown that makes us feel superior and makes the other party look stupid. Especially if we don't get along with that other person, it can be tempting to consider. In times like that, I pause and consider for a moment if it were me who was the one:

- Being shamed;
- Being proven wrong in front of an audience; or
- Made to look stupid;

How would I respond/feel?
Probably defensive, angry, and hurt.

Usually, our best responses are not rooted in defensive, angry, or hurt emotions.

Before you take your aligned action, ask yourself these final gut-check questions:

- Is there a more creative alternative I could consider?
- Is the action based in fear?
- Will I regret what I do next?
- Have I considered the outcomes?
- Will this have a long-term impact? Is it permanent or temporary?
- Would I be happy if someone did this to me?

Taking aligned action means it's aligned with and considers everything you've processed so far using the RAINA Method.

CHAPTER 4

Example Applications

In this chapter, I will share a few of my own experiences to help illustrate how to apply these steps.

My Sister's Wedding

The Facts:

My sister got engaged on New Year's Eve 2019.

Her wedding date would have been sometime in the Fall of 2020.

Then in March 2020, a Worldwide Pandemic happened.

The Wedding Date was changed to 4.3.21 or April 3rd, 2021.

A Difference of Opinion:

During the planning process, my sister voiced that she would prefer there not be masks in her wedding pictures.

At the time, my family was regularly wearing masks. I had a lot of anxiety around this and around attending a large gathering during this time.

Where It Could Have Gone:

This very easily could have ended badly.

My sister and I live 5 minutes from each other and are very close. We both felt the intense strain on our relationship.

I considered not going to her wedding. I was heartbroken, frustrated, and upset to have to choose between feeling safe and honoring my sister's wishes.

My sister was frustrated and angry with me because she felt like I didn't support her and what she wanted for her big day.

If we had let it end that way, I think we both would have regretted it.

Thankfully during this time, unbeknownst to me, I was in the throes of developing the RAINA Method.

This heartbreaking conflict with my sister would lay the groundwork for this method and this book.

RAINA Method Application:

R - Assume they're **Reasonable** and valid

I tried saying to myself, "Of course that makes sense. It's totally reasonable that from my sister's point of view, she would prefer not to wear masks.

She doesn't want to look back on her wedding day and be reminded of COVID-19 in every single picture."

A - Amplify their position

I asked myself, "In her world, how would this be a simple truth?"

If it were my wedding pictures, I could understand not wanting to wear masks. I would want to see people's faces.

I asked myself, "Why might that be?" "What would it have to look like for her to say and act that way?"

I told myself that if it were my wedding, I would probably save money and get married on Zoom.

However, I challenged myself to really consider if that were true. I also thought more about my sister and her situation.

I thought about her age, her health, her friends, and how that might affect her interactions with others.

She was the last of her friends to get married. My sister is one of the most maternal people I know. She's always taking care of others, and I know she's always wanted to be a mom.

So I considered how hard it must be to watch all her friends get married and start having kids without her.

She watched and attended all of their weddings as maid of honor and bridesmaid. I know she spent tons of money and time planning their bridal showers and bachelorette parties.

She probably had years to think about what hers would be like. I know she had wanted to go to Europe or New York for her bachelorette party. Those plans eventually got scrapped.

During that time, she also found out that four of her bridesmaids were pregnant, limiting what some of them were able to or interested in doing for the wedding and the activities leading up to the big day.

At this time, I had already been married for ten years, so I tried to remember what the planning process was like and how stressful it was trying to balance everyone's needs and requests.

I realized it was probably stressful normally, but layer COVID-19 on top of that and it was probably exponentially more stressful trying to plan.

I - **Inspect** and investigate your biases

After amplifying her position, I was already starting to feel a little less combative.

I asked myself these questions to uncover some of the common biases that arise when we disagree with an opinion:

"Am I trying to prove I'm right?"

Yes, I was. I kept sending her articles and safety guidelines that outlined the importance of masks and vaccines. I felt like it was just a matter of providing enough evidence.

"If I'm not trying to defend myself, is there some truth to the statement?"

Yes, if I wasn't trying to convince her about mask safety, then I could concede that her wedding was going to be outdoors and maybe the masks were not totally needed. Plus, more and more data was being released as time went on, so maybe we didn't need them as much.

"Do I feel like I need to defend my behavior?"

Yes, my daughter was doing distance learning, and my husband and I were working from home, so we weren't really out in the world. If we did go out, we wore masks. And we were not attending many, if any, social functions.

"Am I looking for validation?"

Yes, I talked to anyone that would listen about my bridezilla of a sister. I wanted other people to confirm that what I was asking for was reasonable.

"Am I carrying any shame around this? Around being this or around doing this?"

Yes, I did. I felt totally uncool and very conservative compared to others. Even my parents had both decided to attend and wanted all their siblings to attend as well. I definitely felt like the odd person out, and therefore felt like maybe I was overreacting or being unreasonable in comparison.

"If I'm not ashamed of my behavior, can I just own this truth?"

I originally wasn't going to include this example because I didn't want to write anything polarizing.

But the truth is that I believe in vaccines, and I believe in wearing masks, so I will just own that truth.

"If I wasn't feeling attacked, how would I respond?"

If my sister's words didn't feel like an attack on my character and my choices, then I would probably be vulnerable and tell her how scared I really am.

I would tell her how much I love her and how much I want to attend her wedding, but that I have an irrational fear that everyone we love will get COVID-19 and die if we get together and don't wear masks.

"Am I responding in a passive-aggressive or sarcastic manner?"

I've definitely been told I have a death stare and an inappropriate tone to my voice when I disagree with you. So yes, I probably didn't convey my feelings in a light, kindhearted manner.

"What is most important to me when making a decision?"

Family is the most important thing to me, as a priority for the way I live my life and as a core value.

If that holds true, then I had more thinking to do, as my actions from this would greatly affect critical familial relationships in the future.

"What kinds of information or opinions do I value? What kinds do I dismiss? And why?"

I value scientific findings and evidence-based facts. Numbers and statistics speak to me.

I've always been an overthinker, someone who follows logic versus someone who follows their heart.

"What are my main sources of information? What news sources, podcasts, and people do I listen to? Do those sources of information have people or entities that they criticize or dismiss? Have I watched/read those other sources of information directly with an open mind?"

I followed the Centers for Disease Control and Prevention and the World Health Organization. I also relied on my husband's opinion. I did force myself to watch a number of videos shared by my Instagram followers, who were anti-vaccine and anti-mask.

For those who felt we were overreacting with the masks and quarantining, I watched what they had to say with an open mind.

Prior to creating this method, I would not have taken the time to seek out or watch content produced by people I did not agree with. I would have dismissed it as rubbish without even looking at it.

Watching this content did not change my mind on vaccines, but it did give me insights into why some people are anti-vaccine. It helped me understand their perspective better. I find when I can understand better, I can empathize and hold space for other opinions I might disagree with.

"What kind of mood am I in right now? What state of mind? Am I unhappy right now?"

Pretty awful, depressed, and anxious. I wanted my sister to exhibit that she was feeling that too, but to me, she seemed aloof and cool as a cucumber which seemed to upset me more. I found her reactions to be incongruent with the level of threat I felt COVID-19 presented to our family's health and safety. Based on that, I felt like she didn't grasp the gravity of the situation.

N - Uncover Your **Naked Truth** - What do I really want? What is a mutually beneficial goal?

I really wanted to attend my sister's wedding without being fearful of people getting sick.

I also wanted her to have a dream wedding because she deserved to have her special day.

I asked myself these questions to see how close I was to my naked truth and finding a mutually beneficial solution for all involved:

Will other people be affected by how I react?

Yes, I believed my parents would be in an awkward position if I didn't attend. We're all very close.

Plus, I was making the decision for my spouse and daughter.

If I did not attend, then they also would not attend. If I did attend, it would mean they would attend, and if they got sick, I would feel that it was my fault.

How could I see the situation differently?

I'm a planner. I planned my entire wedding almost a year before it happened. It's very hard for me to have plans changed at the last minute.

My sister is much better at rolling with the punches. Maybe if I could just have faith that it would all work out, I could lessen my anxiety level.

Perhaps, I could just wait to see what the recommended guidance was closer to the wedding date instead of pressuring my sister to make a decision now.

Am I open to a solution I cannot yet see?

Yes, even though I could not see it, I wanted there to be an alternative that worked for all.

Am I solving the issue to the benefit of both parties? How about for the benefit of all parties affected?

I initially wanted to wait and see what the mask mandate would be when her wedding date came, but I eventually concluded that I would attend her wedding regardless because she was too important to me to miss it.

Would both parties likely be better off than they were before our interaction?

Yes, if I could take my mask off for pictures, then my sister would be very excited and grateful because everyone else had already agreed.

A - Take **Aligned Action**

I asked myself these questions about the action I planned to take:

Is there a more creative alternative I could consider?

I couldn't think of one but I knew my sister was exhausting all avenues trying to think of how to make the event as safe as possible, while also still making it a dream wedding for herself.

Is the action based in fear?

Yes, not attending her wedding would most certainly be a decision made based in fear. Whenever a potential action is based in fear, I try to pause, because I truly believe we are not our best selves when we act from a place of fear.

Will I regret what I do next?

I would forever regret not attending my sister's wedding, even more than getting COVID-19.

Have I considered the outcomes?

I did consider the outcomes. One would be possibly losing my relationship with my sister, and I was not willing to risk it.

Both my parents agreed to attend, so they were taking the risk.

Will this have a long-term impact? Is it permanent or temporary?

Yes, wearing the masks in the pictures would have a long-term impact on my sister.

Wearing or not wearing a mask to her wedding would be a temporary event experience, lasting no longer than a day. Though if someone contracted COVID from the event that could have both short and long-term impacts depending on the severity.

Would I be happy if someone did this to me?

If I didn't want people to wear masks in my wedding photos, and they did it anyway, it would really upset me.

I had to ask myself this for the multiple options I was considering at the time to help me decide what I wanted to do.

In summary, the Aligned Action I planned to take was to talk to my sister and tell her that I would wait to see what the mask mandate would be as it got closer to her wedding date, but that ultimately I would attend her wedding regardless because she was important to me.

So Here's How It Went Down:

After a lot of self-reflection, I had a heart-to-heart with my sister both in person and via FaceTime.

I shared it all:

- I shared what I thought her stance was based on my assumptions.
- I shared my own personal reflections on the issue and shared where I was self-aware.
- I shared my naked truth and the ideal outcome I wanted that I felt was mutually beneficial to us both.

It was messy. There were lots of tears.

My sister validated some of the assumptions I had for her position and clarified some things I had not considered.

For instance, she shared that she was not aloof and detached because she was cool as a cucumber.

She was actually very aware of my feelings but was making decisions based on the information available at the time, balancing that information with her and everybody else's desires for the wedding, and ultimately hoping for the best.

She only seemed impartial because she had already made her peace with the possible unfortunate consequences of her decision to not have guests wear masks during pictures and to not further postpone her wedding due to the pandemic.

She shared with me all the conflicting concerns and requests she was fielding from our parents, her future-in-laws, and the other potential guests, including all the things she had put into place to ensure the environment was as safe as possible because she too had her own hesitations.

We cried over the fact that I might not attend.

I cried because I really wanted to attend, but I was deathly scared and I was worried she would never forgive me.

She cried because she didn't want to force me to not wear a mask when she knew how scared and uncomfortable it would make me.

She would rather I not be there than have that stress hanging over her all day on what should be the most magical day of her life. She said even though she would miss me not being there that our relationship was more important, and while sad, she was really okay, if I decided I couldn't come.

We didn't argue much about it after that heart-to-heart.

And when the date finally came around, I did attend the wedding. We did not wear masks in the wedding pictures, and thankfully, no one at the wedding got sick.

Looking at her wedding album, you would never guess it took place during a pandemic. It was so beautiful, and my sister said it was absolutely perfect.

Okay, let's do a quick summary recap:

The RAINA Method

R - Assume they're **Reasonable** and valid

I assumed that it was reasonable and valid for a bride to want no masks in her wedding photos.

A - **Amplify** their position

I put myself in my sister's shoes to understand how long she had been waiting to get married and how many other concessions she had to make because there was a pandemic.

She knew it might be a big ask, but she also had hope that it would all work out.

I - **Inspect** and investigate your biases

I definitely was coming from a place of fear. I am naturally a worrier and am always planning for the worst-case scenario.

I recognize that my best behavior is not rooted in fearful emotions.

N - Uncover Your **Naked Truth** - What do I really want? What is a mutually beneficial goal?

I really wanted my sister to have the wedding of her dreams. She deserved it after she was in everyone else's weddings and hosted everyone else's wedding showers and bachelorette parties.

I wanted everyone to be happy and healthy, and most importantly, I wanted to maintain the relationships in my family.

A - Take **Aligned Action**

I decided not to come from a place of fear. I also laid off asking her for updates and trusted she would make the right decisions with the information available at the time. I put our relationship first and decided regardless of what happened, I wanted to be there for her. I also had a heart-to-heart with her and shared my hopes and fears honestly.

As a result, my sister got the wedding of her dreams, our relationship is stronger than ever, and everyone that attended was able to stay healthy.

Online Hate

The Facts:

I use Instagram to host live sales as my primary business model versus a traditional online web store. Live sales are where you stream online in real-time and customers buy the products by typing in the comments section.

As I became more successful in running my business, I also became a bigger target for online hate and criticism.

One person, whom I'd never interacted with before, posted in her Instagram stories that some businesses create a false sense of scarcity and urgency to buy when they sell in live sales.

She then included a screenshot from one of my live sales as an example.

A Difference of Opinion:

I love selling via live sales on Instagram. It gives me a chance to interact live with my customers, and I believe it creates a sense of community being able to hang out like that.

I've also found live sales to be very efficient and a format that goes really well with my lifestyle and my family's needs. For these reasons, I feel that selling via live sales on Instagram is an ideal method of doing business.

However, not everybody agrees with me. In this instance, this person believes live sales should not be used as a format for selling a product because they believe it can create a false sense of scarcity and urgency to buy.

Where It Went:

By this time, I had developed a version of the RAINA Method and had learned to openly address criticism in the form of an Instagram post when it came to my business. Doing so was in alignment with what I had processed through the Raina Method and met the needs of my business and my values.

So, I ended up making a post about it. I did not specifically identify her and titled it, "So, someone called me unethical and another ridiculous. Let's talk about it."

RAINA Method Application:

R - Assume they're **Reasonable** and valid

I could see her point that live sales could create a false sense of scarcity and urgency to buy.

There's scarcity because you feel like what's on the table is all there is. Period. Even though there may be plenty available in many other places.

There's urgency because if you don't comment fast enough, someone might beat you to it.

A - **Amplify** their position

I asked myself, "In their world, how would this be a simple truth?"

I saw that she had previously hosted live sales. Perhaps, they didn't go well and left her with a negative experience.

Maybe she had customers complain about them. She might be the type of buyer who likes to thoroughly research her buying options ahead of time and not be rushed. Thus, she might want to provide her customers with a similar buying experience.

I - **Inspect** and investigate your biases

Before responding to the story she posted and the DMs I received, I sat with the feedback and asked myself these questions to uncover some of my biases:

"Am I trying to prove I'm right?"

Yes, I am still fairly convinced live sales are the best way to sell.

"If I'm not trying to defend myself, is there some truth to the statement?"

When I stopped trying to defend what my choices were, I could see some truth in her statements.

"Am I looking for validation?"

At first, I was looking for outside validation that I was a good person and that my business decisions were good and fair. After stepping back and thinking about it, I stood behind my business decisions and decided that I didn't need validation for that. I only needed validation from myself and through processing these thoughts, I had it.

"If I wasn't feeling attacked, how would I respond?"

I decided writing a post about it and being really open about my business practices is how I would respond. Her "attack" was just a perfect opportunity to address why I sell via live sales.

"Am I responding in a passive-aggressive or sarcastic manner?"

This one is always hard. There's always room for improvement. Sometimes, I'll run it by my husband first to catch where I might have "tone" in a post or message. I know my first response is not always my best response, so that's why I always try to pause and process how I'm feeling through this method first.

"What is most important to me when making a decision?"

At the end of the day, I always want to be thoughtful and intentional. I want to be open to feedback, but not so open that I'm constantly changing directions. So, this method helps me process the feedback in the most unbiased way I can.

And from that place of peace and calm, I can decide if there's some personal development opportunity for me to grow or perhaps a business decision, process improvement, or other action that needs to be made or not made.

"What kinds of information or opinions do I value? What kinds do I dismiss? And why?"

I value the opinions of those I wish to be like. I value the opinions of those who have reached a type of success that I would like to reach.

I take advice with a grain of salt if it's from someone who has not walked in my shoes or achieved what I wish to achieve.

I recognize that those opinions can still have value, even if the delivery is hard to swallow. It's why I developed this method. Processing the opinions of others through the RAINA method strips away the noise of an imperfect delivery or hateful commentary to find constructive feedback to make myself better.

N - Uncover Your **Naked Truth** - What do I really want? What is a mutually beneficial goal?

I really wanted to address why I do live sales. I have found a lot of success through my business model, and I genuinely wanted others to find similar success. I didn't want the gatekeeping I had encountered when I started my business.

Ideally, people would agree with me, but I know that's not a realistic goal. This taught me to get comfortable with some people not agreeing with me and maybe even, not liking me because of it.

Will other people be affected by how I react?

Yes, other people would be affected by how I react, in the event, I reacted publicly.

Am I solving the issue to the benefit of both parties? How about for the benefit of all parties affected?

I feel that I did the best I could with the situation. When someone is not open to hearing your opinion or they're a stranger online, I think it's okay to walk away from the conversation. I had no previous relationship with her and did not plan to have one in the future. If it had been a loved one that I cared about, I probably would have invested more time and consideration and made an effort to talk to her directly.

In regards to solving the issue to the benefit of both parties, I could have easily publicly called her out and told her all the ways I thought she was wrong, but I didn't. When I was feeling petty, I fantasized about coming up with the perfect comeback, but I felt that was unnecessary and would only contribute to more negativity.

I did not feel any further interaction with her would have been productive. I don't think anything I said would have made us besties or even left her liking me more afterwards. And if that was the case, then to me, there was no reason to prolong the dialogue or to senselessly argue.

A - Take **Aligned Action**

Given everything above, I decided to write the post as an inspirational learning opportunity. It allowed me to talk about my business and the way I run it and why. I wanted to create something positive out of the negative experience.

It was my intention that other small business owners who read it would be left feeling empowered and seen. For my current customers and future potential customers, I wanted them to get a flavor of how I deal with criticism and conflict. I believe you can tell a lot about a business based on how they respond to an unsavory "review".

Is the action based in fear?

Not talking about why I do live sales would have been based in fear. I recognized that if I didn't own my business model then I would be coming from a place of shame or fear about what others would think.

Will I regret what I do next?

If I had gotten into a public fight with this person, I recognized that I would regret it. I didn't want to argue with someone that I was probably just going to agree to disagree with.

Have I considered the outcomes?

I did go through several drafts and scenarios in my head about what I would say, where I would post it, and how I would prove that I was right, but I eventually landed on writing a post and just using the opportunity to acknowledge the other opinion while owning my own thoughts on the matter. It was important to me not to publicly shame her or get petty.

Will this have a long-term impact? Is it permanent or temporary?

How I responded to this criticism could have a long-term impact on how my customers view me and my business.

The interaction itself was temporary.

Would I be happy if someone did this to me?

Yes, considering the alternatives. If I publicly called out a large business, I would hope they would respond by addressing the issue I had contention with as opposed to attacking me for bringing it up.

This is a great example of how the RAINA Method allows us to make it about the issue and not about the other person.

Okay, let's recap:

The RAINA Method

R - Assume they're **Reasonable** and valid

I assumed it was reasonable and valid for her to feel that live sales should not be used as a method to sell products because it might create a false sense of scarcity and urgency to buy.

A - **Amplify** their position

Based on her experience and how she runs her business, I could understand why she feels it's an unfair practice to sell via live sales.

It was also potentially something she wanted to bring attention and awareness to by posting about it. Maybe in her mind, she was looking out for her customers and wanted to make sure they didn't overpay or fall for the false sense of scarcity and urgency that live sales can create.

It was also probably helpful to give a very specific example of someone practicing it.

I - **Inspect** and investigate your biases

I definitely had a different background than her and some biases about how to run a business. The need to be right is always a strong bias I have to acknowledge.

N - Uncover Your **Naked Truth** - What do I really want? What is a mutually beneficial goal?

I really wanted to address what I felt was an unfair call out, but address it in a way I felt good about. I wanted to address the issues without getting into a fight with the other person.

A - Take **Aligned Action**

I feel writing the post the way I did was aligned with what I had processed about the issue using the RAINA Method. The post addressed the issues but did not attack the person which was my goal. I felt proud of the way I responded because it was much more intentional and thoughtful than my first gut-instinct response would have been.

Working Mom Woes

The Facts:

I live in San Diego, CA with my husband and daughter.

When my daughter was born, I was lucky my mom lived nearby and was available to watch my daughter during the day when I went to work.

My mom would have my daughter in her care, on average, from 7:00 a.m. - 6:00 p.m., five days a week.

A Difference of Opinion:

My mom and I have different parenting styles and rules in our homes.

I gave instructions to my mom on my preferences for my daughter's care.

I would grow frustrated at the end of the day. When I picked her up, I would hear things like she mostly had fast food and sweet treats all day, "because she wouldn't eat anything else, and she needed to eat something."

Or I would find out that her homework had not been done and that I needed to help her with a project that was due tomorrow.

I always felt relegated to the bad guy role. It felt like my mom got to do the fun stuff during the day and I got the leftovers. It was always a little touchy because my mom was watching her for free, so I didn't want to complain or come off as unappreciative. So I felt I had to pick and choose my battles.

Where It Went:

For about 7 years, both my mom and I suffered, unbeknownst to each other.

I cried regularly, as a working mom with feelings of guilt and failing at motherhood.

My mom is not a crier, but I know I often did not express my frustrations until they boiled over. So I often was pretty worked up, when I would give feedback on how unhappy I was.

I know I can come off as condescending at times, and I imagine she felt defensive and possibly belittled when I would start listing everything that was bothering me.

We eventually had a heart to heart that was facilitated by my sister, but I wish I had this method sooner.

And actually, during the process of writing this book, we revisited this time in our lives. We had even more insights and revelations to share with each other. So, I have discovered it's never too late for healing past emotional wounds.

So let's go through it in retrospect, for some additional insights.

RAINA Method Application:

R - Assume they're **Reasonable** and valid

In retrospect, I could see that my mom's decisions and actions were reasonable and valid, from her point of view, at the time, and in the moment. My mom was the one in the trenches during the day with my daughter and likely saw and experienced things I had no insight into. To her, she was doing what needed to be done to give the best care to my daughter.

A - **Amplify** their position

My mom loves my daughter and only wants the best for her. I imagine she probably did her best to keep my daughter happy and occupied during the day.

I can only imagine the battle it was over food or even homework, as I still experience the struggle now with my daughter, many years later.

My daughter has a strong personality and lots of energy, so I imagine it might have also been a tiring day watching her from 7:00 a.m. to 6:00 p.m.

I - **Inspect** and investigate your biases

Here are some questions to uncover some of my biases:

"Am I trying to prove I'm right?"

Yes, I thought I knew it all. I thought my mom just needed to be firmer. Let my daughter go hungry if she does not want to eat what is provided at mealtime. Tell her she can't play games or go on her iPad until her homework is done.

"If I'm not trying to defend myself, is there some truth to the statement?"

Yes, now that I work from home and I'm with my daughter a whole lot more, I realize it's a whole lot easier said than done when it comes to pretty much everything.

My mom would try to explain how the day went or why they went off track. I recognize I was not always actively listening though because I was frustrated about what was outside my control.

"Am I looking for validation?"

Yes, I was definitely looking for validation that I was a good mom. I got that at work through accolades or raises, but I lacked that at home. No one praises you or gives you good feedback about your role as a mom.

"Am I carrying any shame around this? Around being this or around doing this?"

Yes, I felt bad that I liked going to work and that being a mom did not come naturally to me. I believed my mom to be the best mom in the world when I was growing up. She was so amazing and fun. I felt like I could never live up to her, and I felt ashamed of my shortcomings.

"If I wasn't feeling attacked, how would I respond?"

Sometimes, if my daughter was upset when I came to pick her up, my mom would ask me what I was doing with her when she wasn't in her care. It definitely felt like a personal attack because I already felt deficient as a mom.

If I wasn't feeling attacked, I could probably see that my mom was perhaps just concerned for my daughter's well-being. Maybe in her mind, asking me several questions was a way of deducing what could be wrong. And through her line of questioning, she could possibly help by giving me additional advice.

"Am I responding in a passive-aggressive or sarcastic manner?"

Yes, when I was feeling attacked and hurt, I definitely became defensive and sarcastic in tone or I'd roll my eyes and give my mom a glare. It didn't help that I have narcolepsy and have suffered from chronic sciatic nerve pain in my back over the years. When I am tired and hurting physically, I am not my best self.

"What is most important to me when making a decision?"

Family is really important to me. I love my mom and daughter more than anything, and in addition to getting along personally with my mom, I want them to have a good relationship too.

While I sometimes verbally spar with my mom, I also want her to know how much I appreciate her and what she does for our family. When I am feeling like a bad mom, I am not always good at expressing my gratitude and love toward her.

I recognize now that the guilt, from working and feeling like a bad mom, made me super defensive in my interactions. If I had been able to see that, I would have been able to focus on the real issues of troubleshooting what was working and not working for my daughter's care.

N - Uncover Your **Naked Truth** - What do I really want? What is a mutually beneficial goal?

I really just wanted to be recognized as a good mom, and I wanted my mom to feel good as a caregiver for my daughter. I also wanted to have a good relationship with my mom, as well as raise my daughter to be happy and healthy.

Will other people be affected by how I react?

Yes, my dad, sister, and husband often got caught in the crossfire when my mom and I were fighting. Not only would they have to listen to us rant about each other but also be our shoulders to cry on because it hurt to be fighting.

How could I see the situation differently?

My mom may have felt like I was condescending and talking to her like a child when I would describe why I was frustrated with some of her actions and when I would say what my expectations were in contrast.

I believed my mom thought less about me for working so much, so I was feeling less than adequate as a mom.

While I was feeling deficient, perhaps she felt underappreciated and infantilized by my words.

If I had been able to put my feelings aside, I believe it would have really changed how I approached our conversations.

Here's How It Could Have Gone Down:

If I had used this method when this all happened, I believe I could have stayed more level-headed. Yes, it would still have been frustrating, as parenting is hard.

I believe I would have responded better in the moment and been better able to recognize how I was feeling and ask for what I needed. Maybe I could have seen that we needed to be a parenting team rather than on different sides of an issue.

Let's do a quick recap:

The RAINA Method

R - Assume they're **Reasonable** and valid

I could have assumed that my mom was reasonable and valid in the choices she made for my daughter's care.

A - **Amplify** their position

I could have imagined what it was like in her shoes to struggle with getting my daughter to eat healthy food choices and get her homework done in a timely manner every day.

I - **Inspect** and investigate your biases

I could have realized I was feeling deficient as a mother and that I was taking that out on my mom.

N - Uncover Your **Naked Truth** - What do I really want? What is a mutually beneficial goal?

I wanted my daughter to have the best possible care. I wanted my mom to feel confident and happy in her experience taking care of my daughter. I also wanted to feel like a good mom and know that my mom felt I was a good mom too.

A - Take **Aligned Action**

I needed to have a heart-to-heart with my mom and express my naked truth with her. Once we realized we wanted the same things, it was easier to connect and empathize with the struggle. We were able to talk it through without getting defensive or feeling hurt. Her reading of this book gave us a common language and terms to use that helped guide our conversation.

Don't give up. In the next chapter, we'll discuss more on how to practice what you have learned.

CHAPTER 5

How to Practice

The RAINA Method is designed to help you keep your cool so that you do not get provoked into an argument, regrettable behavior, or an unproductive hate/blame cycle of pointing fingers.

It can be difficult and unnatural at first, but like all things, with practice and repetition, it gets easier and, over time, can become second nature.

One of the best ways to learn the method faster is to teach and share the method with someone else.

Or even recapping it for yourself, if you do not have someone to share it with.

Another way to learn this is to mentally walk through it for a situation in which you are not involved and don't feel heated about.

This allows you to practice showing empathy for both sides.

You can also do this on interactions that have already taken place.

This practice will help you learn the method, making it easier to recall and apply in the moment.

Progress will be shortening the time between the event or interaction with someone, and when you apply the method.

At first, you might use the method a couple days after an interaction with someone.

Then perhaps, a few hours after.

Then one day, you'll actually be able to apply it in real-time.

Observe how it changes your responses over time.
Notice how more in control of your thoughts and feelings you are.

Notice how the other person reacts.
Discover new possible outcomes.

In my personal experience, it's been much more favorable in both cases.

I've felt better, less anxious, and more peaceful.

I've also noticed the other person responds in a more positive or neutral way, versus if I had responded in a defensive or attacking manner.

If you find the RAINA Method helpful, help someone else.

Share this book.

Carry it around in public. Talk about it with those around you. Spread it because you believe in a kinder world.

Display it on your desk at work, so it can be an easy talking point.

Bring it up in conversation and share how using it has personally helped you.

KEY TAKEAWAYS & ADDITIONAL EXERCISES

HOW TO USE THIS SECTION:

It is my hope that you might carry this book around with you in your purse, car, or briefcase for easy access.

Instead of thumbing through the entire book, I want you to be able to flip to the back for easy reference to some of the common questions and exercises for each step.

I recommend using them as journal prompts for more expanded reflection.

May they leave you feeling more confident and peaceful for having used them.

The RAINA METHOD

R - Assume they're **Reasonable** and valid
A - **Amplify** their position
I - **Inspect** and investigate your biases

N - Uncover Your **Naked Truth** - What do I really want? What is a mutually beneficial goal?

A - Take **Aligned Action**

R - *Assume they're* ***Reasonable*** *and valid*

Try saying to yourself, "Of course that makes sense. It's totally reasonable that from their point of view they would think that."

A - **Amplify** their position (Includes Additional BONUS Exercises)

Try saying, "In their world, obviously that makes sense. If I grew up with friends and family who taught me that, and the only life experience I've had has not shown me otherwise, then why would I believe differently?"

Ask yourself, "Why might that be?" "What would it have to look like for that person to say and act that way?"

Think about their age, their race, their health conditions, their residence, and how that might affect their interactions with others.

BONUS EXERCISES

Another exercise that might help is this:

1. Tell the Story from your point of view. You're the Hero/ Protagonist, right?

2. Now retell the Story from their point of view. How would it sound if they were the Hero/Protagonist and you were the Villain?
3. Imagine them sitting with their friends or partner as they share their side of the story. What does it sound like?

Say aloud, "I am open to thinking differently about this. I am open to other viewpoints. My experience is not the only experience."

The energy with which you do this will decide how successful you are at truly empathizing with the other person and seeing things from their point of view.

If you approach this with hate, resentment, or pessimism, you've already clouded the possibilities of success.

I constantly reset and intentionally put myself in the best state to do this.

Some example states or positions I try to think from might be:

- From a loving point of view. Unconditional love for yourself and for the other person. A kind, gentle voice.
- From a place of gratitude. Recognizing I might have privilege and that others may not.
- From a place of mindfulness. Coming from a place of observance, detachment, and awe.

Still struggling to understand their point of view?

Ask yourself this, "Am I saying it's absolutely impossible for someone to feel this way?"

Obviously, the answer is "no", since someone is feeling this way.

So what could that possibly look like? Where would one even start? What would life have to look like for someone to believe that?

Here are some questions to ask yourself if you're still running into mental roadblocks:

- How much have I traveled and experienced other places and cultures different than my own?
- How many cultures have I lived in?
- How many levels of income have I lived through?
- How much hardship have I survived?
- Am I disabled or have health conditions that impair my daily life?
- Have I ever been discriminated against?
- Have I ever been judged unfairly?
- What questions or circumstances have I not considered?
- What resources, mentors, or voices could I consult to expand my understanding?
- Am I saying it's impossible to do anything to further my understanding or compassion?

These questions are also not valid excuses for anything.

This is not a comparison game to judge other people, but rather an exercise to become aware of possible biases and differences between your experience and the experience of others.

I share these because much of our anger, when we disagree with someone's opinion, usually stems from the fact that we think they made the wrong decision or choice.

We rationalize or assume they had the same choices as us. And in that situation, we would have done something different.

We forget to pause and realize, their choices are not the same. Their experience is not the same as ours.

It is presumptive to assume and yet we do. We do it all the time.

And in some cases, maybe they truly do have similar choices to us, but:

- Certain responses have never been modeled for them by people in their lives.
- It's intentionally not being chosen by them.
- It would be unsuccessful if attempted due to other extenuating circumstances or conditions.

Let's challenge ourselves to consider why someone might have valid reasons for their opinions. Why, in fact, in their world, their opinions and conclusions might be completely obvious.

Sometimes, we don't know what we've never experienced or been exposed to, and it's severely lacking to judge someone or something without having all the information.

I - *Inspect* and investigate your biases

Ask yourself these questions to uncover some of the common biases that arise when we disagree with an opinion:

- Am I trying to prove I'm right?
- If I'm not trying to defend myself, is there some truth to the statement?
- Do I feel like I need to defend my behavior?
- Am I looking for validation?
- Am I carrying any shame around this? Around being this or around doing this?
- If I'm not ashamed of my behavior, can I just own this truth?
- If I wasn't feeling attacked, how would I respond?
- If what they're saying didn't comment on my life choices, then how would I feel?
- If what they're saying is true, does it imply I'm a bad person?
- Am I responding in a passive-aggressive or sarcastic manner?
- What is most important to me when making a decision?
- What kinds of information or opinions do I value? What kinds do I dismiss? And why?
- What are my main sources of information? What news sources, podcasts, and people do I listen to? Do those sources of information have people or entities that they criticize or dismiss? Have I watched/read those other sources of information directly with an open mind?
- What kind of mood am I in right now? What state of mind? Am I unhappy right now? Is my mood clouding my response?

- Am I making a blanket statement or generalization about a group of people?
- Am I blaming or defending a group of people?

Here are some questions to ask yourself to aid in objectivity:

- Have I attacked or blamed a person or group of people for something?
- Am I willing to concede to being wrong?
- Do I have to be right?
- Am I afraid of being wrong?
- Am I too attached to a specific outcome to be objective?
- Have I considered the state/country infrastructure, laws, or systems in place that might be playing a large role in the other person's world? Or play a large role in mine?
- Is there a power or privilege differential between me and the other person? Do I have shame around that difference? If I have power and privilege, can I own or use them to both our advantage?

N - Uncover Your Naked Truth - What do I really want? What is a mutually beneficial goal?

Ask yourself these questions to see how close you are to the naked truth and finding a mutually beneficial solution for all involved:

- Will other people be affected by how I react?
- How could I see the situation differently?
- Am I open to a solution I cannot yet see?
- Am I solving the issue to the benefit of both parties? How about for the benefit of all parties affected?

- Are both parties better off than they were before our interaction?
- Am I considering the larger/whole picture?
- Am I considering the infrastructure of our society and culture?

A - Take *Aligned Action*

Ask yourself these questions about the action you plan to take:

- Is there a more creative alternative I could consider?
- Is the action based in fear?
- Will I regret what I do next?
- Have I considered the outcomes?
- Will this have a long-term impact? Is it permanent or temporary?
- Would I be happy if someone did this to me?

A Note From the Author

I'm so grateful for my loved ones who have helped me edit this book and who have believed in and supported me every step of the way. I could not have done it without them.

And to you, thank you so much for reading my book. I'm so humbled and honored that you're here.

I hope you're better off for having read it. It's my wish that the RAINA Method brings you much peace and calm around otherwise very tough issues.

Sending you lots of abundance and good vibes.
With love,
Raina

Made in the USA
Monee, IL
16 March 2023

d43d1ff6-86cf-4933-b4a2-0895dbad56c7R01